إيزيسُ وأوزيريسُ

Isis and Osiris

Retold by Dawn Casey

Illustrated by Nilesh Mistry

Arabic translation by Wafa' Tarnowska

Mantra Lingua

في اليَوْمِ الَّذِي وُلِدَ فيه أوزيريسُ رَنَّ صَوْتٌ في أعالي السَّموات قَائلاً: "إنَّ إلَهَ كُلِّ الأشْياء قَدْ جَاءَ إلى العالَمَ". بَعْدَ يَوْمَيْنِ فَقَطْ وُلِدَ أخُوهُ ستْ.

كانَ الأخَوَانِ مُخْتَلِفَيْنِ جِدًّا؛ إذْ كانَتْ بَشَرَةُ أوزيريسَ سَمْرَاءَ داكِنَةً مُشْبَعَةً مِثْلَ السَّهْلِ الخَصِبِ. لكِنَّ وَجْهَ ستْ كانَ أحْمَرَ وَشاحِبًا مِثْلَ الصَّحْرَاء المَيّتَة. كَما أنَّ أوزيريسَ كانَ يُحِبُّ السَّلامَ وَستْ يُفَضِّلُ الحَرْبَ.

On the day that Osiris was born a great voice rang out from the heavens: "The Lord of All Things has come into the world."

Only two days later his brother Set was born. Never were two brothers so different. Osiris' skin was dark and rich like the fertile plain. Yet Set's face was red and sallow as the lifeless desert. And while Osiris loved peace, Set preferred war.

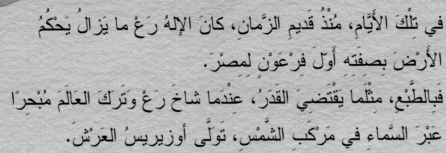

في تِلْكَ الأيّامِ، مُنْذُ قَديمِ الزَّمانِ، كانَ الإلهُ رَعْ ما يَزالُ يَحْكُمُ الأَرْضَ بِصِفَتِه أَوَّلَ فِرْعَوْنٍ لِمِصْرَ.

فَبِالطَّبْعِ، مِثْلَما يَقْتَضي القَدَرُ، عِنْدَما شاخَ رَعْ وَتَرَكَ العالَمَ مُبْحِرًا عَبْرَ السَّماءِ في مَرْكَبِ الشَّمْسِ، تَوَلَّى أوزيريسُ العَرْشَ.

At that time, so very long ago, Ra still ruled on Earth as the first Pharaoh of Egypt. And, sure as fate, when Ra grew old and left this world to sail across the skies in his boat-of-the-sun, it was Osiris who took his throne.

أَصْبَحَ أُوزِيرِيسُ وَزَوْجَتُهُ إِيزِيسُ مَلِكَ وَمَلِكَةَ مِصْرَ. حَكَمَاها بِالحِكْمَة وَالصَّلَاحِ، وَحَلَّ السَّلَامُ عَلى الأَرْضِ كُلِّها. حِينَئِذ زَارَ أُوزِيرِيسُ العَالَمَ كُلَّهُ يُعَلِّمُ النَّاسَ الَّذِينَ كانَ يَلْتَقِي بِهِمْ. كانَ السَّلَامُ يَحِلُّ أَيْنَما ذَهَبَ. في غِيَابِهِ كانَتْ إِيزِيسُ تَحْكُمُ بِحَزْمٍ وَبَرَاعَة عَلى بِلادِ مِصْرَ. عِنْدَما عَادَ أُوزِيرِيسُ مِنْ سَفَرِه عَمَّتِ الفَرْحَةُ لأَنَّ كل رَعِيَّته كانت تُحبّه ... كُلُّهُمْ إِلّا واحِدًا فَقَطْ ...

Osiris and his wife Isis became Pharaoh and Queen of Egypt. They ruled wisely and well. Peace prevailed throughout the land.

Then Osiris travelled the whole world teaching the peoples he met. Wherever he went, peace followed. And while he was away Isis reigned over the land of Egypt with strength and skill.

On his return there was great rejoicing, for all his people loved him.

All except one…

... أخوه سِتْ.

ويوْمًا بَعْدَ يوْمٍ، وَسَنَةً بَعْدَ سَنَةٍ، كانَ سِتْ يُرَاقِبُ أَعْمالَ أخيهِ البِكْرِ بِغَمْطٍ في عَيْنَيْهِ وَغِيرَةٍ في قَلْبِهِ. وَكُلَّما كانَتِ الهُتافاتُ المُتَوَجِّهَةُ إلى أوزيريسَ تَرِنُّ في أُذُنَيْهِ، كانَ الحِقْدُ يَكْبُرُ في قَلْبِهِ. لِذلِكَ دَبَّرَ خُطَّةً لِيَقْضِيَ بِها على أَخِيهِ إلى الأَبَدِ.

…his brother Set.

Day after day, year after year, Set watched his elder brother's good deeds with scorn in his eyes, and jealousy in his heart. Now, as the cheers for Osiris rang in his ears, Set's hatred burned, and he devised a plan to destroy his brother forever.

سِرًّا، أَمَرَ سِتْ أَنْ يُصْنَعَ لَهُ تابوتٌ جَميلٌ مُزَخْرَفٌ بِأَجْمَلِ الزّينَةِ الأَنيقَةِ
الرَّقيقَةِ يُلائِمُ حَجْمُهُ جِسْمَ أوزيريسَ.

أَقامَ سِتْ حَفْلَةً فَخْمَةً عَلَى شَرَفِ أوزيريسَ حَضَرَها سِتْ مَعَ أَتْباعِهِ. هُناكَ
عَرَضَ التّابوتَ أَمامَ الحاضِرينَ فَشَهَقوا وَتَعَجَّبوا وَسُرُّوا كَثيرًا بِرُؤْيَتِهِ إِذْ أَنَّهُ
كانَ يَلْمَعُ مِنْ كَثْرَةِ الفِضَّةِ وَالذَّهَبِ وَاللّازَوَرْدِ، كانَ أَزْرَقَ مِثْلَ سَماءِ اللَّيْلِ
وَكانَتِ الأَحْجارُ الكَريمَةُ فيهِ تَتَلأْلأُ مِثْلَ النُّجومِ.

Secretly Set had a beautiful casket built. It was exquisitely decorated, and it was just the right size to fit Osiris' body.

A royal feast was held in Osiris' honour. Set was there with his followers. And there, he presented the casket. The guests let out gasps of wonder and delight at the sight of it. It shone with silver, gold and lapis lazuli, blue as deep as the night sky, and precious gems sparkled like stars.

ثُمَّ أَعْلَنَ سِتْ: "مَنْ يُلائِمُ حَجْمُهُ حَجْمَ هذا التَّابوتِ يَكونُ لَهُ هَدِيَّةً."

أَخَذَ الضُّيوفُ يُجَرِّبونَ التَّمَدُّدَ في التَّابوتِ ضاحِكينَ وهازِلينَ. تَمَدَّدُوا فيهِ واحِدًا بَعْدَ الآخَرِ، لكِنْ كانَ واحِدٌ كَبيرًا والآخَرُ قَصيرًا والآخَرُ سَمينًا والآخَرُ نَحيلاً. لَمْ يُلائِمِ التَّابوتُ أَحَدًا أَبَدًا.

أَخيرًا جاءَ أوزيريسُ قائِلا: "دَعْني أُجَرِّبُ." دَخَلَ في التَّابوتِ وتَمَدَّدَ. كانَ بِمَقاسِهِ بِالتَّمامِ.

"Whoever fits inside this casket shall have it as a gift," Set announced.

Eagerly the guests entered the casket, laughing and joking. One by one they lay down in the chest, but one was too tall, another too short, one was too fat, another too thin. Not one man fitted into the chest.

And then, Osiris came forward. "Let me try," he said. He stepped into the casket and lay down. It fitted perfectly.

بُمْ..! صَفَقَ سِتْ الغِطاءَ وَأَقْفَلَهُ جَيِّدًا. فَحُبِسَ أوزيريسُ داخِلَهُ.
وَبِسُرْعَةِ الرِّيحِ المُعْصِفَةِ جاءَ أَتْباعُ سِتْ وَطَرَقُوا المَسامِيرَ في التّابوتِ وَأَغْلَقوهُ جَيِّدًا.

BANG! Set slammed down the lid and snapped it shut, and Osiris was trapped inside. Swift as the storm wind Set's followers rushed forward, and hammered the coffin closed.

بِدَفْعَةٍ قَوِيَّةٍ رَمَى أَتْبَاعُ سِتْ التَّابوتَ في نَهْرِ النّيلِ وَابْتَلَعَتْهُ المِياهُ الدَّاكِنَةُ. وَهكَذا انْتَهَتْ حَياةُ أوزيريسَ الطَّيِّبِ.

With an almighty splash Set's followers flung the coffin into the Nile,
and the dark waters closed above it.
And so ended the life of Osiris the good.

عِنْدَمَا اكْتَشَفَتْ إِيزِيسُ ما قَدْ حَصَلَ لِزَوْجِها الحَبِيب، بَكَتْ دُمُوعًا مُرَّةً. لكِنْ مِنْ خِلالِ دُمُوعها عاهَدَتْ نَفْسَها بِهذا القَوْل: "الرِّجالُ يَمُوتونَ لكِنَّ الحُبَّ يَبْقى. سَوْفَ أُفَتِّشُ مِصْرَ كُلَّها عَنْ أوزيريسَ حَتّى أَعْثَرَ عَلَيْه." كانَتْ إِيزِيسُ تَعْلَمُ أَنَّ رُوحَ أوزيريسَ لَنْ تَكونَ أَبَدًا حُرَّةً لِتَدْخُلَ "دوات"، أيْ بِلادَ الأَمْواتِ إلّا إِذا أُقيمَتْ طُقوسُ الجَنازةِ الصَّحيحَةُ.

بَدَأَتْ إِيزِيسُ بَحْثَها. وَما أَنْ تَرَكَتِ العَرْشَ حَتّى اسْتَوْلى عَلَيْهِ ست. كانَ حُكْمُهُ جائِرًا فَظًّا، وَاضْطُرَّتْ إِيزِيسُ أَنْ تَلْجَأَ إلى مُسْتَنْقَعاتٍ وَأَدْغالِ الدِّلْتا. هُناكَ وَلَدَتِ ابْنًا لأوزيريسَ أَسْمَتْهُ حُورُسَ.

أَرْضَعَتِ الأُمُّ ابْنَها بِحَنانٍ. لكِنَّها كانَتْ تَعْلَمُ أَنَّهُ إِذا عَثَرَ عَلَيْهِ ست، لا بُدَّ أَنْ يَقْتُلَهُ. لِذلِكَ وَضَعَتْ إِيزِيسُ ابْنَها تَحْتَ حِمايَةِ إِلهةِ الدِّلْتا اللَّطيفة.

When Isis discovered what had happened to her beloved husband she wept bitterly. But through her tears the widowed queen uttered a vow: "Men die but love lives on. I will search all Egypt for Osiris, and I will find him."

She knew that until the proper funeral rites were performed his spirit would never be free to enter Duat, the Land of the Dead.

Isis began her quest. The moment she was gone Set seized the throne. His rule was cruel and harsh. The good queen Isis was forced to shelter in the swamps and jungles of the delta. There, she gave birth to Osiris' son, Horus. Tenderly the mother nursed her son. But she knew that if Set found him, he would kill him. So Isis entrusted her baby to the care of the kindly goddess of the delta.

هامَتِ المَلِكَةُ في أنْحاءِ المَعْمُورَةِ تَبْحَثُ عَنْ جُثَّةِ أُوزيريس سائِلَةً كُلَّ مَنِ
التَقَتْ بِهِ إِنْ كانَ قَدْ لَمَحَ التَّابُوت.
لَمْ تَتَوَقَّفْ مَرَّةً لِتَرْتاحَ ولَمْ تَفْقِدِ الأَمَلَ أَبَدًا.

The queen wandered far and wide seeking the body of Osiris, passing no one without asking them if they had caught a glimpse of the chest.
Not once did she rest. Never did she give up hope.

فَتَّشَتْ لِمُدَّةٍ طَوِيلَةٍ دُونَ جَدْوَى إِلَى أَنِ الْتَقَتْ يَوْمًا جَمْعًا مِنَ الْأَوْلَادِ كَانُوا قَدْ رَأَوْا الصُّنْدُوقَ يَعُومُ عَلَى النَّهْرِ الَّذِي يَصُبُّ فِي الْبَحْرِ، وَقَدْ حَمَلَتْهُ مِيَاهُ الْبَحْرِ الْجَارِيَةِ إِلَى شَوَاطِئِ لُبْنَانَ، حَيْثُ أَلْقَتْهُ الْأَمْوَاجُ تَحْتَ جِذْعِ شَجَرَةِ أَثْلٍ صَغِيرَةٍ. لَكِنَّ الشَّجَرَةَ مَا لَبِثَتْ أَنْ كَبُرَتْ وَامْتَدَّتْ وَطَالَتْ وَلَفَّتِ التَّابُوتَ دَاخِلَ جِذْعِهَا إِلَى أَنِ اخْتَبَأَ كُلِّيًّا. ثُمَّ كَبُرَتِ الشَّجَرَةُ وَطَالَتْ وَأَصْبَحَتْ قَوِيَّةً ذَاتَ رَائِحَةٍ زَكِيَّةٍ. فَذَاعَ خَبَرُهَا وَسَمِعَ عَنْهَا الْمَلَكُ. وَعِنْدَمَا رَآهَا قَالَ آمِرًا: "اقْطَعُوهَا! أُرِيدُ أَنْ يَكُونَ جِذْعُهَا عَمُودًا فِي قَصْرِي!" وَهَكَذَا، مَكَثَ التَّابُوتُ وَاقِفًا دَاخِلَ الْجِذْعِ، عَمُودًا فِي قَصْرِ الْمَلَكِ، بَقِيَ سِرُّهُ فِي دَاخِلِهِ بِأَمَانٍ.

For a long time she searched in vain, until one day she met a group of children. They had seen the chest floating down the river and away out to sea. The swift waters had carried it to the shores of Lebanon, where the waves had gently set it down to rest at the base of a young tamarisk tree. The tree quickly grew up around the casket, enfolding it within its trunk until it was completely hidden.

The wonderful tree grew tall and strong and aromatic. Its fame reached the ears of the king himself, and when he saw it he commanded, "Chop it down! I shall have it as a pillar in my palace!"

The trunk stood in the king's palace, a magnificent pillar, its secret still safe inside.

أَسْرَعَتْ إِيزِيسُ إِلَى لُبْنَانَ فِي الْحَالِ. هُنَاكَ صَادَقَتْ خَادِمَاتِ المَلِكَةِ وَأَخَذَتْ
تُدَرْدِشُ مَعَهُنَّ بِحَرَارَةٍ وَتُرِيهِنَّ كَيْفَ تَجْدِلُ شُعُورَهُنَّ.
سُرَّتِ المَلِكَةُ جِدًّا وَدَعَتْ إِيزِيسَ لِتَمْكُثَ فِي القَصْرِ.

Isis rushed to Lebanon at once. There, she befriended the queen's maids, chatting warmly, and showing them how to plait and braid their hair. The queen was enchanted and invited Isis to stay in the palace.

لكنَّ الخادِماتِ أخْبَرْنَ الْمَلِكَةَ أنَّ إيزيسَ كانَتْ تُخْرِجُهُنَّ كُلَّ لَيْلَةٍ مِنَ الغُرْفَةِ وتُقْفِلُ البابَ، وكُنَّ يَسْمَعْنَ صَوْتًا يُشْبِهُ صَوْتَ زَقْزَقَةِ العُصْفُورِ. في لَيْلَةٍ مِنَ اللَّيالي اخْتَبَأَتِ المَلِكَةُ في الغُرْفَةِ وفَتَحَتْ عَيْنَيْهَا وَاسِعَةً بِدَهْشَةٍ عِنْدَمَا رَأَتْ إيزيسَ تَتَحَوَّلُ إلى سُنُونُوَّةٍ تَطِيرُ حَوْلَ العَمُودِ الَّذي كانَ يَحْبِسُ زَوْجَهَا، وَهِيَ تَصْرُخُ بِحُزْنٍ وكَآبَةٍ.

But the maids told the queen that every night Isis would send them out of the room and lock the door, and they could hear an odd sound like the twittering of a bird.

So, one night, the queen hid in the room. Her eyes widened as she saw Isis transform herself into a swallow, and fly around and around the pillar which held her husband prisoner, uttering sorrowful cries.

ركَعَتِ المَلِكَةُ أمامَ الإلهَةِ إيزيسَ الَّتي كَشَفَتْ عَنْ طَبيعتِهَا الحَقيقيَّةِ،
وَاقِفَةً فَوْقهَا شامخةً مُنِيرَةً.

"أعْظَمُ المَلِكات!" شَهَقَتِ المَلِكَةُ؛ "لِماذا سُمُوّكِ هُنَا؟"

"أرْجُوكِ" تَوَسَّلَتْ إيزيسُ. "أعْطِيكِ بَرَكَتي إذا أعْطَيْتِني العَمُودَ."

حينئذٍ، أمَرَتِ المَلِكَةُ أنْ يُنْزَعَ العَمُودُ. ثُمَّ قَطَعَ أتْبَاعُ المَلِكِ الجِذْعَ
العَظِيمَ وَأخْرَجَتْ إيزيسُ تابُوتَ زَوْجِهَا مِنْهُ وَوَقَعَتْ عَلَيْهِ باكِيَةً،
غاسِلَةً إيَّاهُ بِدُمُوعِهَا.

The queen fell to her knees as the goddess Isis revealed her true form, towering, radiant, above her.

"Ultimate Queen!" the woman gasped, "why are you here?"

"Please," Isis implored, "I will give you my blessing, if you will give me your pillar."

So, an order was sent to take down the pillar. The king's men cut down the mighty trunk.

Isis drew out the coffin of her husband, and fell upon it, and bathed it in tears.

وَضَعَتْ إِيزِيسُ التَّابُوتَ في مَرْكَبٍ وَأَبْحَرَتْ بِهِ.
كانَتْ مُشْتاقَةً لِرُؤْيَةِ وَجْهَ أُوزيريسَ مَرَّةً أُخْرَى، لِذلِكَ، عِنْدَمَا أَصْبَحَتْ وَحْدَهَا،
فَتَحَتِ الصُّنْدُوقَ. كانَ هُناكَ مَيِّتًا. ضَمَّتْهُ إِلَيْهَا وَبَكَتْ وَتَسَاقَطَتْ دُمُوعُهَا الدَّافِئَةُ
عَلَى وَجْهِ زَوْجِهَا الْبَارِدِ.

She placed the coffin in a boat and sailed away with it.
Isis was longing to look upon the face of Osiris once more, and as soon as she
was alone, she opened the chest. There he was. Dead. She held him to her as she
sobbed, and her warm tears fell upon the cold face of her husband.

عِنْدَمَا وَصَلَتْ إيزِيسُ إلى مِصْرَ خَبَّأَتِ التَّابُوتَ في مُسْتَنْقَعاتِ الدِّلْتَا وَهَرَعَتْ لِتَرَى ابْنَهَا.

لكِنْ، لِلْأَسَفِ، في تِلْكَ اللَّيْلَةِ بالذَّاتِ، كَانَ شَخْصٌ يَقْبُعُ في الظَّلَامِ يَتَصَيَّدُ في ضَوْءِ القَمَرِ ...

When Isis arrived in Egypt she hid the coffin in the swamps of the delta while she rushed to see her son.

But alas! On that very night somebody was lurking in the shadows, out hunting by the light of the moon…

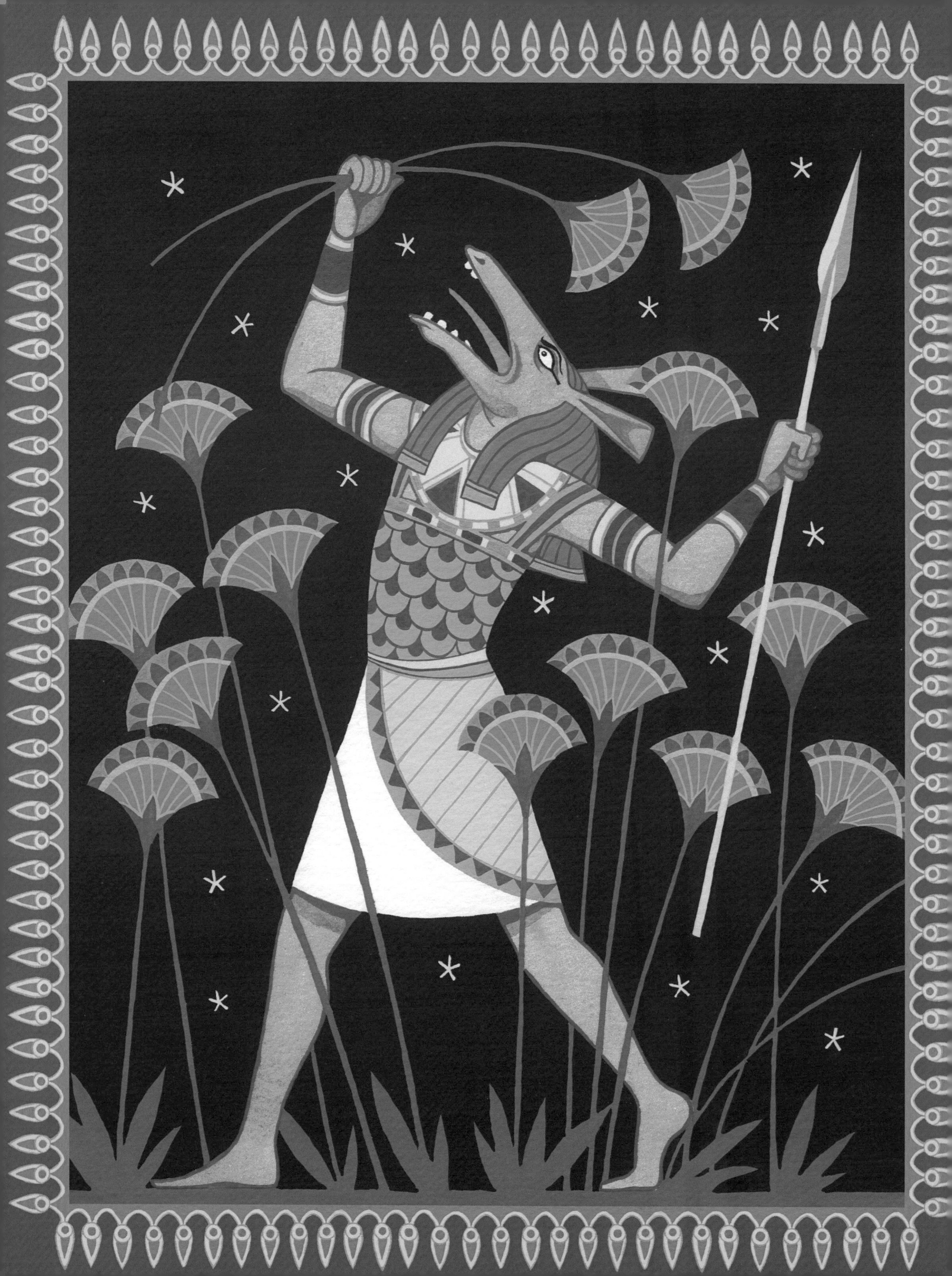

... كَانَ هَذَا سِتْ! عِندَمَا رَأَى التَّابُوتَ عَرَفَهُ فَوْرًا. بِصَرْخَةٍ مُحْتَدِمَةٍ بِالغَضَبِ نَشَلَ سِتْ الجُثَّةَ مِنَ التَّابُوتِ. "لَنْ تَعُودَ هَذِهِ المَرَّةَ!" صَاحَ مُزَمْجِرًا. ثُمَّ قَطَّعَ جُثَّةَ أوزيريسَ قِطَعًا قِطَعًا، وَأَرْدَفَ مُتَجَهِّمًا: "لَنْ تُخَلِّصَكَ ايزيسُ مَرَّةً ثانِيةً!" ثُمَّ رَمَى قِطَعَ الجُثَّةِ الأَرْبَعَ عَشْرَةَ في جَمِيعِ أنحَاءِ مِصرَ.

أمَّا إيزيسُ التي كَانَتْ قَدْ عَانى قَلْبُهَا الكَثِيرَ، والتي كَانَتْ قَدِ انهَمَرَتْ دُمُوعُها مِثلَ المَطَرِ، ذَرَفَتِ الآنَ دُمُوعًا تَكفِي لِيَفِيضَ النِّيلُ. هَل تَتَخَلَّى عن حبيبها في آخِرِ الأَمْرِ؟

…Set! When he came across the coffin he recognised it at once.

With a howl of rage he snatched the body from the chest.
"This time you will not return!" he roared, and he ripped
Osiris' body limb from limb. "Isis will not save you again!"
he snarled, and he scattered the fourteen pieces over the
length and breadth of Egypt.

Isis, whose heart had already endured so much,
and whose tears had already fallen like rain,
now wept tears enough to flood the Nile.

Would she give up at last?

كَلاّ أَبَدًا! صَنَعَت المَلِكَةُ لِنَفْسِها مَرْكَبًا مِنْ وَرَقِ البَرْدِيِّ وَأَبْحَرَتْ فيهِ إلى مُسْتَنْقَعَاتِ النّيلِ باحِثَةً عَنْ قِطَعِ جُثَّةِ زَوْجِها الغالية.

قِطْعَةً قِطْعَةً جَمَعَتْها إيزيسُ. قِطْعَةً قِطْعَةً ضَمَّتْها إلى بَعْضِها البَعْضِ، ثُمَّ جَلَستْ هي وَأُخْتُها نِفتيسُ إلى جانِبِ الجُثَّةِ تَنُوحانِ بِأَعْلى صَوتَيْهِما على نَفْسِ المَلِكِ المَقْتُول.

ارتَفَعَ صَوتاهُما إلى السَّماءِ حَيْثُ سَمِعَهُما إلهُ الشَّمسِ رَعْ فَأَشْفَقَ على إيزيسَ وَبَعَثَ الإلهَيْنِ أنوبيسُ وتوتَ لِيُساعِداها.

مَعًا لَفُّوا الجُثَّةَ وَضَمَّدُوها. ثُمَّ حَنَّطُوها بِالمَراهِمِ والدُّهونِ. هكذا صُنِعَتْ أوَّلُ مُومِيَاءَ مِصرِيّة.

Never! The brave queen made a boat for herself from papyrus and sailed the swamps of the Nile searching for the precious pieces of her husband's body.

Piece by piece Isis gathered up the broken parts. Piece by piece she laid them back together.

Isis and her sister Nepthys sat beside the body and sang loud laments for the murdered king. Their wailing reached as high as heaven, and up in the skies the Sun-god Ra heard their cries, and he took pity on Isis. He sent the gods Anubis and Thoth to help her.

Together they swathed the body in bandages. Together they embalmed it with ointment. Thus Egypt's first ever mummy was made.

ثُمَّ عَقَدَتْ إِيزِيسُ تَعْوِيذَةَ سِحْرٍ قَوِيَّةً لَمْ يَكُنْ
قَدْ خَبَرَهَا أَحَدٌ مِن قَبْلُ. وَمَا إِنْ رَفَعَتْ
ذِرَاعَيْهَا إِلى الأَعْلَى حتى تَحَوَّلَتا إِلى
جَنَاحَيْنِ بَهِيَّيْنِ. ثُمَّ حَامَتْ فَوقَ الجُثَّةِ تُهَوِّيهَا
بِرِيشِ جَنَاحَيْهَا. اندَفَعَ الهَوَاءُ لِيَدْخُلَ
مِنخَرَيْ أُوزيريسَ الذي تَنَشَّقَ الهَوَاءَ
وَتَنَفَّسَ من جديدٍ.
هكذا أَصْبَحَتْ رُوحُ أُوزيريسَ حُرَّةً أَخيرًا.
فَذَهَبَتْ إِلى عَالَمِ الأَمْواتِ الذي حَكَمَ عَلَيْهِ
أُوزيريسُ كَمَلِكٍ وقَاضٍ إِلى آخِرِ الدَّهرِ.

Then Isis performed a powerful magic, such as had never been seen before. As she raised her arms they were transformed into a pair of glorious wings. Isis flew above the dead body, and as she fanned her feathers the wind from her wings rushed into Osiris' nostrils, and he inhaled, and breathed again.

And so the spirit of Osiris was free at last, and it passed into the Land of the Dead. There he ruled as Judge and King for all eternity.

عَادَتْ إِيزِيسُ إِلَى دِلتَا النِّيلِ لِتُرَبِّيَ ابْنَهَا الطِّفْلَ. عَلى مَرِّ السِّنِينَ، أَصْبَحَ حورُسُ رَجُلاً قَوِيًّا وَشُجَاعًا وَكَانَ مَلِكَ مِصرَ الحَقِيقِيَّ.

كَانَ أَبوهُ أُوزِيرِيسُ يَزورُهُ مِرَارًا مِنْ عَالَمِ الأمواتِ وَيُعَلِّمُهُ فُنُونَ المُحَارِبِ، إِذْ كَانَ حُورُسَ يَنْوِي أَنْ يَثْأَرَ لِأَبِيهِ قَبْلَ كُلِّ شَيْئٍ آخَرَ.

بِقَلْبٍ ثَابِتٍ، عَزَمَ حُورُسُ ابْنُ إِيزِيسَ وَأُوزِيرِيسَ أَن يَهزِمَ عَدُوَّهُ.

Isis returned to the river delta to bring up her baby son. As the years passed, Horus, the rightful king of Egypt, grew into a strong and brave young man. Osiris often came to him from the Land of the Dead, and taught him the skills of the warrior, for above all else Horus hoped to avenge his father.

With a firm heart Horus, son of Isis, heir of Osiris, set out to defeat his enemy.

احتَدَمَتِ المَعرَكَةُ عِدَّةَ أيامٍ. قالَ البَعضُ إنَّ حورُسَ طَلَبَ مِنَ الآلِهَةِ أَن تُعطِيَهُ القُوَّةَ وَتُساعِدَهُ، فَتَحَوَّلَ إلى قُرصٍ نارٍ مُلتَهِبٍ يَشِعُّ مِثلَ الشَّمسِ وَلَهُ أَجنِحَةُ نارٍ مَمدودَةٍ. بَهَرَ الشُّعاعُ جُيوشَ سِتْ وَأصابَهُم بِالعَمى فَارتَبَكوا وَأخَذوا يُحارِبونَ بَعضُهُم البَعضَ!

The battle raged for many days. Some say Horus called on the power of the gods to help him, and was transformed into a blazing disc, as bright as the sun, with outstretched wings of fire. Blinded by the brightness, Set's armies were dazzled and confused and they began to attack one another!

لَكِنْ لَمْ يَكُنْ التَّغَلُّبُ على سِتْ سَهلاً فَقَد اسْتَنْجَدَ بِتَعْويذةٍ سِحْرِيّةٍ قَوِيّةٍ
من عِنده حَوَّلَتْ جُنُودَهُ إلى جَيْشٍ مِنَ الجَواميسِ النَّهْرِيّةِ والتَّمَاسِيحِ
التي انْزَلَقَتْ بِصَمْتٍ إلى النِّيلِ مُتَرَقِّبَةً مُرُورَ مَرْكَبِ حُورُسَ. مَا إِن
انطَلَقَتْ سَفِينةُ حُورُسَ حتى بَدَأ رِجالُهُ يَسْتَعِدُّونَ لِلْمَعْرَكَة. قَوَّوْا
رِماحَهُمْ وسَلَاسِلَهُمُ الحَدِيدِيّةَ بِعِبَارَاتٍ سِحْرِيّةٍ، ولَمّا رَمَوُا السَّلَاسِلَ
في الماءِ نَشِبَتْ في أَطْرَافِ وقَوائِمِ الحَيَوانَات. ثُمَّ جَرُّوا الحَيَوانَاتِ
وطَعَنوها بِرِماحِهِمِ المَسْنُونة وشَقُّوا جِلْدَهَا. عِنْدَمَا رَأَى سِتْ أَنَّهُ
قُضِيَ على حَيَوانَاتِه هاجَ غَضَبًا وهَزَّتْ صَرْخَاتُهُ الأرضَ كَالرَّعْد؛
أَقْسَمَ قَائِلاً: "سَأَقْتُلُ حُورُسَ بِنَفْسِي". ثُمَّ تقدَّمَ نحوَ حُورُسَ كوَحْشٍ
شَنِيعٍ ذِي رَأْسٍ ذَميمٍ يَقْطُرُ مِنْهُ دَمٌ خَائِرٌ نَتِنٌ.

But Set was not so easily defeated; he called on fierce magic of his own, transforming his men into an army of huge hippopotami and crocodiles. Silently they slid into the Nile, lying in wait for Horus' boat.

As Horus sailed up the river, his men prepared. Their lances and chains were crafted of iron, but they were strengthened with spells.

The men cast their chains into the water, entangling legs and limbs. They dragged the bellowing beasts towards the sharp points of their lances and pierced their skins.

When Set saw his beasts destroyed, his cries of rage shook the earth like thunder. "I will kill Horus myself," he swore, and changed his form again - he advanced on Horus as a hideous monster, with stinking gore dripping from a rotting head.

بِضَرْبَةٍ وَاحِدَةٍ قَطَعَ حُورُسَ رَأْسَ سِتْ ثُمَّ قَطَّعَ جِسْمَهُ قِطَعًا قِطَعًا.
وَقُضِيَ عَلَى فِسْقِ سِتْ أَخِيرًا. وهكذا انْتَصَرَ حُورُسُ وجَلَسَ لِلْمَرَّةِ
الأُولَى على عَرْشِ أَبِيهِ وَحَكَمَ بِحِكْمَةٍ وَصَلَاحٍ مِثْلَ مَا حَكَمَ أَبُوهُ
أوزيريسُ مِنْ قَبْلِهِ.

With a single slice Horus cut off the head, and hacked the body to pieces. The wickedness of Set was quenched at last.

Horus was triumphant, and so for the first time sat down on his father's throne. And Horus ruled as wisely and as well as Osiris before him.